# Between Here and There

## Words n Such

BY CHRISTINE CURTIS

CURTISY PUBLISHING GROUP

Copyright © 2017 by Christine Curtis.
All rights reserved. This book or any portion thereof may not be reproduced or used in any manner whatsoever without the express written permission of the publisher except for the use of brief quotations in a book review.

Printed in the United States of America

First Printing, 2017

ISBN-10:0692981977

Creative Director and Designer:
Charity Coleman

Editor:
Ashley Singleton

Curtisy Publishing Group

A division of Innovation & Execution Enterprises, LLC.
Baltimore, MD 21229
CurtisyPublishingGroup@gmail.com

---

**www.TheChristineCurtis.com**

At 19, I wrote a 150-piece collection of poetry and never published it.

Due to my battle with self-doubt and depression, I decided to leave the work out of the hands of the public. Then, in an act of frustration, I deleted every last poem. Since then, life has bestowed many lessons upon me. The most important lesson I have learned is that life will give you nothing if you give life nothing; withdrawals require deposits. This current collection is my deposit. It is my method of defense against depression, self-doubt, frustration, and anything else that would prohibit me from living a life that I desire to live. My hopes, my dreams, and my aspirations are all wrapped in stanzas and covered in honesty. This is my way of giving back to the universe what I have been fortunate enough to acquire. What you will ultimately find is a secure, aware, bothered, weak, yet strong, transparent, and vulnerable me. You will unequivocally find my truth. Nothing more, nothing less.

The mind is a mysterious and miraculous entity.
I am amazed at what it holds onto over time.
I want to thank all those who have played a role
or two in my life.
This is because of you...

## **NIGHT GAZES**

In the dark.
In the night.
Glimmers of the street lights,
Caresses of the breeze from the humidity
covering the trees, my window, my eyes,
And I wonder where you are.
My heart longs for you.
Just you.

Maybe mannequins that embody your speech.
Your frames I picked out for him hoping he
could become a remake.
But it's really still,
Always has been.
Always will be you.
I pray for you.

To be happy in her arms, hoping her love feels
better than mine.
Hoping that memories fade like the color of the
shades hiding the rays that the sun left imparted
on my skin, reminding me it was here...
Yeah, there.

I hope you forget me.

But still it's you.
I find bits of you in everything.
In him, it, days, books, songs, smells, tastes,
touches, sounds, as my feet touch the ground

I think and have always thought of you.

I search for you.
A recent photo.
A new look to still feel connected.
I wish you to never come back.
I am and have metamorphosed into
A 180 you won't recognize.
My heart beats differently following the little
heart's songs I once ignored.
You and I were one in a time where I didn't
know me.
I was running from me.
I wasn't free.
But I was dying to be...
To be me.

But it's still you.

But you won't even see me if you saw me today.
So forget me but don't regret me.
Pray that my heart cries for someone else as it
still does for you.

## STRANGERS

. . . . . .

She saw him but her eyes recognized not his figure.
Nor the brown specs that lie in the creases of his eyes.
His voice didn't ring in her ears and his scent
did not beckon her to a memory.
It was not destiny.
It was an occurrence.
It was a moment of two souls, through pupils pierced,
greeting each other so that she knew he was kindred.
He didn't stop to think or be anything but, present.
He was and her soul relaxed in the moment.
And she knew she felt his gaze before.
She sat and allowed the spirits to mingle and in one glance,
after the dancing of two minds finalized and the moment
dissipated, that she knew.
The spirit of the previous "him" had moved to him.
His look caressed her heart.
It was sweet like cavity infected teeth
devouring cotton candy.
Sweet like sugar scrubbed lips.
Like loves first kiss full of what if's.

This was it.
The woman said,
"Ask yourself, could you fall in love with a stranger?"

"Came close to beating the communion out of my cries."

*In the Affirmative*

## QUEEN

Shades of nude, neutral, or natural do not
measure your beauty, because your lips sparkle
in the sun with each ray that's reflected off your
balm-beat pillows.

Your curves are invaluable and not because
they are ample or they are lacking or nonexistent.
They are precious simply because they sit on you,
in whatever size they are, regardless
of what condition they are in.

Your hair isn't only deemed perfection by the
definition of coiled kinks curated perfectly with the
twist, product, and finger twirling method that you
practiced all day to make.

Your divinity isn't defined by the materials on
your back or by the style they're in.

You are divine simply because you inhale and exhale.
You are a walking inspiration.

## CHILDISH

I pray that when I step on the crack I don't
break her back.
I wonder what she would say if she knew
these thoughts.
I wonder if she could really feel.
Maybe that's why she's mad at me.
I wonder if she even really remembers me.
I'm too old for games now,
but these past times keep me connected to her.
These past times.
These childish games are all I have of good
memories for that's all she is.
I can't say God rest her soul because
she still resides on this side of the ground.
She's still around,
physically weakened by life's grasp;
a grasp she was never able to fight off.
She's still fighting though,
more than anything herself,
and her thoughts,
and her voices.
I am the enemy in her mind because time
has convinced her that I am not who I say I am.
I am doing better than most of my family combined.
On an island amongst them.
Still never able to win.
So at 30, I play.
I dream and think things I wish I could say.
And I pray that when I step on the cracks
I never break my mother's back.

"Because you love it when I coo.
Sweet sounds and melodies
Making declarations of your work down hallways."

***Voice Recognition in Love***

## COLORS

A term handpicked for deception.
Divisive in nature.
The creator never spoke these words,
yet we refuse to recognize the hidden lies.

## SECRETS

If they only knew
my reserves couldn't even satisfy because so much ice
has built up, not even the melting droplets could cure.
My distaste for need and addiction to new has me in two,
between my thoughts and you.
Maybe three or four
And only one knows of all.
No promises have made for commitments.
No vows shared but I feel like an adulterer.
I only want what I want from them.
I only need them for it.
Outside of that I have me.
I only need me.
If they only knew what they couldn't see.

"Let me feed you.
Fixings liking to your palette.
Fit for a king."

**Dinner Time at Your House**

## BLACK EXCELLENCE

. . . . . .

Perfect.
Unbreakable.
Undeniable.
Composition of gold and precious metal,
you are divinity.
Your very presence is deemed grand.
Whatever you touch
becomes historic.
Call yourself.
Name yourself.
Define.
Create.
Build after being broken yourself.
You.
Are.
The very definition itself.
Falter.
Shift.
Collapse Not.
You are the very foundation.

## PLASTERED CONVERSATIONS

If these walls had inner voices,
and made outer noises,
the rhetoric would be so blasphemous,
your poor little religious heart would tear down
this room to the ground.
See my stories aren't pretty or witty.
They're lines
thrown together to appease none.
So you'd say how many fucks were given?
This paint would tap dance in freedom to finally tell my dirt
of how many people I ripped from my hip of friendship and
didn't even bat an eye.
Why? Cause good things don't hurt inside.
So swayed to the rhythms of texts messages,
conveying buyer's remorse;
an investment now wasted in their opinions.
Conversations where I listened with intent,
intending not to offend,
ending up only begging to amend.
So I stopped.
Shut the door to complacency.
Ended all ties with apologies and stopped belittling me.
to appease the agony or arrogance I never claimed property of.

If these walls had voices
their hearts would scream of defeat.
Another one bites the dust and I turned it into a sugar scrub.
Crazy.
Bitter.
These terms often spewed in anger to me and I laughed no

matter the color of the tears.
If these walls had voices, they'd say I honestly lost all religion and even the jeans don't fit me anymore.

"He needs specific words to be spoken at specific times in order to feel justified."

*Necessity*

## UNKNOWN

. . . . . .

I see you in my dreams.
Form fitting to the descriptions given, hidden and exposed in the word and in the world
You are my foreword and all of my after thoughts.
I faint not waiting for you to be what I know you will be.
I know.
Though we have never walked down the same street, our eyes never been trapped from across a room, your scent has never grazed the nostrils, striking my memory glands to keep your pace embedded in my brain and me reminiscent of our nonexistent first conversation...
I know you.

## MOTHER'S LAST SEED

I managed to tuck you away.
Fitted in crevices never fitted for the evidence
of things not seen.
Imagination can't run wild for it's founded in
sanity.
But your voice rings like a new bell when
familiar freckles become focused.
And my pivots less potent.
I can see you in my dreams.
You follow me even more.
Nevermore to the core will your love
come thru my door
Why come?
For?
Shoved away begging for crumbs off your
kitchen floor.

"Bargain with eternity,
offer up my peace and soul."

***On My Knees***

# FIXED

I'm broken.
Let's start with that.
Bent into shapes,
carved into places and things,
built destructively and poetically to justify
the eternal juxtaposition of the arguments between he and me.
But I provide no voice for the wrongdoings.
I speak for the foundation.
Of fist fights and larynxes used to battle the air waves which
competed with their illogical and irrational reasoning.
I, with my own eyes, mimicked patterns and thought processes
deemed to be the reality.
I was fed,
turned it into an elixir and subdued my soul with solitude and
selfishness to only find me here, in pieces.
A soliloquy at best.
Regret timbers at my door.
And I'm bombarded with reflections.
Shattered glass, my heart, may still be.
Hidden well with warm scents, eloquence, and hypocrisy.
Not looking for a fixer.
Just for a visionary.
Left to suffice with pain and responsibility.
I struggle with compromise and relinquishing.
I don't like my car parked too far just in case I need to flee.
Unaware of a resolution my volumes rise steadily
when the source of the frustration truly has no visibility.

The words may not purse my lips but the fact is
I'm hurting.
Mending is accepted, but understanding is appreciated greatly.

## DEAR MOMMA

I saw you today.
Thick haired,
fair skinned,
faint and familiar to the eyes.
She spoke Spanish.
You and I for a moment were united.
She expressed to me the love she had for her daughter.
How the skies couldn't shine brighter than the seed you bore last.
She had become everything she dreamed and it became too hard for her to share moments with her.
Looking at her reminded her of everything she could no longer be.
Free.
Happy.
Peacefully in tuned with her soul.
She told me she wished I didn't have to make up conversations with you in my mind attempting to live in a moment with you.
She didn't say anything at all, but I imagined she was you.

. . . . . .

"I spoke down to misogyny.

And turned down contradictory doctrines."

. . . . . .

*Big Chop*

## CAN'T LOVE

Cauterized Hearts.
That hurt.
Read a chapter rather page of myself and I cried.
She and I were the same for the few phrases.
Ok there were more.
And the honesty poured from his heart to the pen
to the paper to the hereafter I tried to deny the truth.
Somehow these words were carved from my soul.
They obviously had been cured for years thru visions
and tears and dreams led to fears of failure of
becoming what I swore I was not.
My mother.
I couldn't love him.
I didn't know how.
His love covered my sins.
And I wanted him to run from me.
I couldn't make her see what he saw.
I waited for her touch.
FaceTime is all it was.
His voice "You're making a mistake" rang as I ended what she
and I shared with a text and confident glare at the screen.
I meant what I said or so it seemed.
I couldn't love her either.
I decided to ponder who I was and could not be and
I realized the issue is that I am still scared to love me.
Now this is deeper than mirror, mirror on the wall.
My soul's reflection is effervescent and present in today.
But the girl, the child who was left behind
is still trying to find love.
It has approached me recently.

His calm eased my worries before
confusion crept in and captured my stability.
Maybe it is not me... but it still comes back to me
Never give them more than a week.
Before they make you weak and you're too scared to leave.
So, you sneak out the door leaving a
"Dear John" letter on the floor
because your steady has been captured by his
and you can't even face yourself anymore.
That's what I say.
And sometimes,
few times,
I've decided that people fit into these shapes
without any time passing by.
And I find myself wishing I never hit send or end on that call.
Sometimes,
I wished I never felt their love at all.
It wouldn't be so hard when I leave.
Sabotage your love.
So we can be lonely I say to me.
That's where you're most happy I lie confidently.
I can't love them.
Even if I tried.
Tongue-tied to falsehoods so long that love only runs and hides.

# DEAD OR ALIVE

. . . . . .

Black boy you dead?
You look dead.
You look like a dead man walking with that target on your head.

Black boy?
You afraid?
You look afraid.
You look like you haven't slept in days.
Has your life span decreased with every walk you take?
Has the pain in your eyes increased with every stride you make?

Black boy?
You care?
You know you care.
Or else you wouldn't be fighting these storms while life
continues to form barriers to prevent your greatness from ever
hitting the pavements but wait a minute.

Black boy?
Are you not a King?
You look like a King.
Your ancestors ruled this,
called dibs on everything.
Dressed in jewels with headdresses to proclaim your glory.
Pour me a glass or two 'cause baby when I'm done undressing
you, you're gonna want one for me.

Black Boy?
You're mine.
Your love belongs in The Smithsonian because it has surpassed

the test of time.
I adorn your beauty covered in shades of caramel, mocha, and chocolate.

Black Man?
Are you here?
I can feel you here.
In the middle of my day I send love and light.
I send strength to your back for you're carrying my weight.
I send peace to your mind to keep you sustained while the enemies try to obtain your crown so keep fighting until your oppressor falls down.

My black man
Are you alive?
You look alive
And I will remind you of who you are until the day you die.

. . . . . .

"Starting point: taxi.
Finish line: desk job"

. . . . . .

*The Olympic Commute*

## DRESS UP

I play dress up sometimes with real intentions and uninhibited ambitions,
paying homage to vintage thoughts and future renditions.

## **JOURNEY**

Living life.
Day by day.
Then this fell into our lap.
And we weren't ready.
At the bottom
of the well
We found love.

"Academia could've provided more information,
but I leaned on the jagged edges."

*Black Landscape 1*

## DIVINE

He called her a goddess.
And she turned in the other direction in search
of the recipient of a compliment so potent that
only heaven could conjure up the letters fitting
enough to fulfill the words in it.
She saw chipped paint on her surface
and assumed she was unfit for an upgrade.
He said, "Good morning Queen of Sheba,
Goddess of Aphrodite's womb
from the highest Himalayan mountain top,
born in the Ocean of Oshun!"

And she only walked away...

## **NOTHING**

. . . . . .

You leave me empty.
Hollowed.
Dried out.
No lube.
Nothing.
I'm empty.
You drain what's left
and I let you.
For the sake of scents that ignite my senses, taking me to you.
For the feel of your creative space, I let you invade me.
You have control.
And when it's over.
I'm left with nothing.
You leave me empty and I let you.

"Did your thoughts take you places
unforeseen and reminiscent of us?"

*Long Gone*

## SERVED ON A PLATTER

All it took was one phone call
and you came to me.
Your hunger beckoned me near,
I felt, internally.
No other could satisfy what you need from me.
Feed until you want no more.
Take all of me.

## DINNER

I never asked for your recipes.

Or even your pots and pans.

Never claimed territory to your kitchen
or wanted your dining room table.

I just wanted a taste.

I asked for your generosity before you
thought all I wanted was your sacrifice.

I desired your attention so our souls could dance
together like Misty Copeland as we fed together.

I dreamt you understood my fetish for your heart.

Instead you gathered that I wanted to gather your
image and foundation and change its decorum.

I never wanted your recipes or your dishes,
I just wanted the invite.

"So I bathed in steam.
Poured scalding hot water down my back
while wishing I knew voodoo to provoke your return."

***Where the Water Ran***

## FREE TO FLEE

It's not that I am abandoning you.
I'm just trying to save me.
Currently drowning in murky shallow waters.
Hunted in the dark when you're not here.

## METAPHORS AND MEANINGS

I appreciate the rain.
I don't hide or shy away from it.
I dance with it.
Jump in it.
Recognize its touch.
Stand in its power.
Bask in the middle of the street in its glory.
I'm unafraid.
I don't ask the rain to go home and change
if I am uncomfortable by its beauty.
Umbrellas aren't allowed when she's around.
And when she comes,
I do as well.
I appreciate her.
She is brave.
When the world throws shade she,
nevertheless, makes her presence known.

"Societal norms don't suit my round ass."

*Direct Declarative Statements*

# REQUEST DENIED

No thank you.
I'd rather not.
I'll pass on engaging your toxicity and calling it lunch.
I'd prefer running in the street, meeting an oncoming bus
to impact with my body, forcing me to the ground,
then to sip tea in your company.
You breed pain.
You thrive off pseudo elevation of self to only belittle those
who you consider unequal to your exquisite nature
or so you'd like to think.
Let me skip barefoot on glass.
Glide in agony on pins and needles.
Please, let me dive into shark-infested waters,
jellyfish-saturated waves, killer whale-inhabited oceans
before breaking bread across a small table,
in a quaint intimate restaurant, in an awkward space with you!
You aren't my type of energy.
It's only transferred, never destroyed, and in the past,
you have passed on to me so much negativity
that as I forgave you, I had to forget you.
I'm sorry, who are you again?
Oh yeah...
To your request to drain me,
in response to your question about allowing us to share a
moment, in this present day,
the answer is I'd rather not.
I'd rather be a two bit two-dollar hoe tryna be a thot.
I think not!

## **CONVERSE**

. . . . . .

She paused,
"Yes, I hear you."
She heard him,
but did he hear her?
While he sought to justify his absence as a means to finally solidify their practice, she managed to manage life, once so inclusive of an "Us", now riddled down to an "I".
I can be happy.
I have to change this tire.
I can cry alone because I am ... Alone.
He paused,
"Yes, I hear you."
Her heard her,
but did she hear him.
Closed mouths don't get fed.
But he opened his mouth so many times, the lines were combined with past crimes she regurgitated from past guys because the phrases were conceptualized into facts and so much of them died...
They tried.

"Hogwarts created and spells handcrafted specifically for the specificity of cocoa brown, mocha, toffee, and vanilla-coated embryos to the full-figured sweetly curved goddesses that can only be named as such."

*No Magicians*

## FIND ME

Dense.
Deep.
Beneath the sea.
Treading under.
Moving further.
Come with me.
Shedding tales.
Past scales.
A redefining entity.
Fishing for life.
Beckoning to hide
in your entirety.
Find me.
Where waves crash,
folding at the peak,
rolling beneath our feet.
Where sunrises glide,
and our loves unifies
to create eternity.
Learn me.
Like the corals underneath
pearls firmed to be,
equalize my soul.
Join my energy.

## LOVE ME

Beyond the sand and the beach,
beyond the pretty tides,
further than the outer reach,
find me.
Searching for you,
while I am redefining me.
Keep me safe.
Blind my sight.
Manifest destiny.

"I've played this role before.
I won neither Oscar nor a ring."

*Dance*

## COSMIC TIES

. . . . .

I don't know you,
but I do.
Diamond leveled blue.
Touched by gold.
Magentas and dancing hues;
this is love
or so the song claims it to be true.
You cross my mind.
Like shooting stars do.
And when I find myself gazing in the sky, attempting to locate traces of you,
I replay that shooting star.
So I suppose daily is when I think of you.

## LET YOU

. . . . . .

And so I let you.
Belittled and afraid from days of torture,
torched by a window with light in a bottle,
to only have darkness control my thoughts.
Years later I met you.
Intimidated by what your love cultivated,
I anticipated my escape before the opportunity to conjure up the strength enough to take a sip from your cup.
Bogged down by my tenacity,
I struggled to envision where our visions unified and united.
You and I, I tried to fight it.
But I kept you.
Rather you me.
Verbal assaults unto your heart and mind attempting to push away what you told me was mine.
I aligned myself with a hiatus many times,
calling it space, while I hide behind lies.
And so you let me.
The embodiment of patience,
still by the waters of my soul,
letting me find it so, while apart from me.
Your touch is a part of me.
You still let me explore other territory
Break your heart continuously.
Break down the homes and space we created
and inflated arguments perpetuated without foundation,
using logic outdated.
And then I finally met you.
Tender and vulnerable over and over again,
after moons and stars passed us by many times,

you kept me.
From self-destruction,
self-sabotage,
self-hate,
self-loathe.

"Take one part of the book and forgo the next.
Break my back to bend over parables and fallacies."

***Ode to Righteousness***

## **ALLEGIANCE**

You never existed.
Twisted
in my head.
The lies I speak to keep your spirit
alive not dead.
Somehow,
at night
when I wake up from hot sweats,
drenched in regret,
I see your face.
Literally.
I search for the remnants of your pictures.
No one knows I still hold a shrine.
Your place is on a pedestal,
never to be removed.
Elevated chairman for life.
I can't leave now.
I'm committed.
But I never ceased my dedication,
I'm still devoted to you.

## NECESSITY

. . . . . .

But he needs me.
He needs me more than I need him.

But I need him,
just not in the same measurement.

He needs my support.
He needs specific words to be spoken at
specific times in order to feel justified.

We haven't shared intimacy in a bit but he's content.

Because he needs me
more than I need him.

I need his love.

It's unique.
Vast.
Deep.
Reassuring.

And available.

But I don't need him.

I'm afraid the pool where my love was once held dried up and I
am here wondering where to find it.
I said I would be invested.

So, I vetted my thoughts in search of being "in love"
and I have yet to quench my thirst.

Yet all the while he swims daily in the idea and thought of me.

He finds comfort, without touching me.

He yearns to smell me.

He is happy with my scent in the bed next to thee.

He needs to be had by me.

Unfortunately, it's not reciprocity.
But he knows.

And he finds joy in that void.
Deep and dark.

Tunneling through and from past to possibilities,

I find myself at 1:37am writing expressions while my mind keeps me from finding the same solace easily.

I could leave, but he needs me.

So I sit, unhappy to fulfill what he needs of me.

I stay to keep my word of being invested.

I do so for him.

He needs me to be here
So I stay… reluctantly.

"Divine creation.
Gilded in excellence."

**_Note to Self_**

# RULER

. . . . . .

I don't know that man.

My pen couldn't even,
wouldn't even if it could place his name
anywhere important.

His rhetoric poured out hatred so desperately that I got sick.

Went home.

Thought if I closed my eyes and chugged my vitamins,
that this hallucination of an orange skinned,
weave wearing man becoming the ruler of this freed world
would be remedied with vacation and antidepressants,
because clearly, I was tapping into some other shit.

He ain't my POTUS.
This man never cared about me.

When his father made comments
about disrespecting minorities,

When his wife, an immigrant, was the only
immigrant allowed to be here legally,

When his friends came into the White and ruined our economy,

When his lies stacked up and
towered over the Statue of Liberty and

The EPA was silenced from speaking the truth liberally,

When his hypocrisy and bullying became warning notice
for the UN and México simultaneously,

I knew FOR DAMN sure... I don't know this man.

When his followers attempted to recreate modern day lynching
and were excited by his ignorance
and constant antagonized mentioning,
I wept for this country.

It ain't Fabergé eggs.
It isn't divinity like Misty Copeland's legs
or anything that Maya Angelou has said.

But it's here.
Where my heart resides.
Where babies are created, men are yielded,
and women are born.

It is where we celebrate freedom of speech
and recreating the norm.

Where equality ain't perfect
and sometimes human rights are torn.

But it's here.
And so is he.

And he ain't no president to me.

# INFAT

Is it even possible?
Like legitimately,
factually possible
that I love you?
It can't be.
You're a fantasy.
Fantastical really.
Imagination ran wild,
we already named our unborn child,
you and I found love
in imaginary places,
while my heart races,
after you I see no more.
I wake up.
We couldn't be.
So I'm here.
Wondering.
How much torture could I sit through?
Just to say that I feel you?
Cause I can't possibly love you.
Your middle name is a blur.
The interior decorations of your home never were.
Merely glances of a hand.
An internal dance.
Grasp of my thighs and dark spaces,

With large crowds,
with wide screens,
and moments found.
I'm delusional as fuck.

But this shit is profound.
And yet you're not here.
Instead his love is around.
So I couldn't love you.
There's no way it's true.
What I think I feel.
I share with someone new.

. . . . . .

"You love me until you can't control me."

. . . . . .

**Conditions May Apply**

# COMMUNE

10 years and we still haven't gotten
this communication in alignment.
I mean we speak.
You tap into my soul,
pierce your eyes upon my hearts chamber,
double tap and like my shit,
wishing to kiss my shit,
But that's it; nothing more, nothing less.
Your punctuation invades my pupils,
sending me into an abyss
and I sit.
I create words flowing.
Just like shit like this,
sharing with you shit like this,
your ears always miss
months later you attempt to revive,
what's already dead
and we're back at one.
Leaves fall.
Summer came and gone.
And every winter your love calls my love home.
So we've never ever put our communication in alignment.
I've spent days in tears wondering where our time went.
Why couldn't we fix the error,
errors that destroyed the pair of aligned stars,
set out just for us.
I wished for them and wished on them.
Hoped it would allow your voice to coerce
my love again;
give me a reason again.

But you never communed with my soul,
so the line went dead.

## THE CALM

I trace where glass had wings and flew into walls;
where hearts shattered, and were destroyed.
And there you stood,
Firm.
In your balance.
Unbothered by my winds.

"It was a moment of two souls, through pupils pierced,
greeted each other so that she knew he was kindred."

***Strangers***

## STONE WALL

He chiseled.
His patience grew weary, leery of the daunting task that lay at his feet; me.

## LULLABY

I spend days/
Alone/
Toggling between thoughts/
Enamored by sounds created skillfully amid memories, reminisces, and past lover's faces/
I take to image and use imagery
to carefully depict current statuses/
I take time/
I make time/
Rarely/
I need my mind to not race at night so that in the day/
I won't wander off so quickly mid-sentence in conversations not imperative to the current affairs plastered across pages/
Days and nights are all that's left/
Manmade creation of measurement to masterfully put fear in the hearts of mothers not yet and wives not close to lower esteem not strong enough to withstand the societal norms/
But it's nights that keep me/
I dream both amongst stars and in the company of THEE star/

But nights have me/
Comfort my plans/
Soothe my mourning/
Providing clarity for complacency during the blue skies that only make my mind wander further to sea shores and soft moans I only wished to have repeated/
I spend days/
In solitude/

Unfairly removing people places things/
Unfairly prohibiting those dearest/
I spend nights alone/

But I spend them/
Both equally/
Brilliantly/
Leaving no change behind/
Down to my last penny/
Amid thoughts of you/

"She's still around,
physically weakened by life's grasp;
a grasp she was never able to fight off."

*Childish*

## OH GOD

I find me in you.
You are the thread of my soul.
You are my geyser.
It's your air I breathe.

## ODE TO RIGHTEOUSNESS

. . . . . .

Tell me again to live right.
To be just.
To be modest.
To love one another.
To tithe.
To hide me for God's glory.
To lie.
Lie like I can't read so I must continually
seek the review of the elderly.
Take one part of the book and forgo the next.
Break my back to bend over parables and fallacies.
If the word was before and with and is God,
then why did the word enslave the Gods before it.
Contradictions and definitions provided less clarity.
Pharisees at the table turning their noses down at Jezebels.
Condemning to hell heart-pricked souls yearning for peace.
Tell me again to do what's right.
Use "the word", quote the scripture.

"If they only knew what they couldn't see."

*Secrets*

## INEVITABLE

Stay with me.
Part seas in bed with me.
Create scores of sounds so lovely that angels dance
and memories linger longer lasting past
the due date of this final scene.

Stay with me.
Here.
Just a little longer.
Tamper with imaginary measurements of days.
Recreate visions so that after my scent has faded,
my clothes have since vanished,
and my voice echoes no more against hollowed walls and fine wood floors,
you'll be able to find pieces of me in there
I will be here.
But I can't be here forever.
For the moment partake in Thanksgiving with me.
Let not these last days be bitter, baggage claimed,
or daunting beyond what's necessary.

Find me.

Even in this moment still loving you.
Warm your soul with my endearment.
Caress your heart with my care.

Stay.

Here.

Right now.
For it can't remain.
And nor can I.
Daydream of past times and recent occurrences that don't negate, but prove my love.
Even during uncertain spaces, I was here.
Fully or not, my presence was real.

So stay.
It doesn't have to be painful.
Stay until the morning
and make this ours.

# **DANCE**

I'm asking a lot right?
For us to be aware?
And purposeful?
Is it too much to ask for you to be here?
I keep saying it, but I need it.
You.
To be here.
Cognizant.
Full of intent right now.
I replay ball changes,
shift of hips,
hands sliding up arms,
and across cheeks bones.
Tending to physical expressions of mourning
with pain evident.
To release what's here on to each other,
while we dance.
It's a burden.
I understand.
I've played this role before.
I won neither Oscar nor a ring.
It was bittersweet.
That's the word.
I am asking for limes and sugar canes to graze my lips to yours,
to let kisses and intimacy fade us in to nevermore.
It may be unfair, but it is mine to be had.
It was not as if the lights were not flashing,
but it is not my heartache to define.
So it's too much.
I won't say it.

I pray you don't see it years later.
No regrets,
maybe.
But I wish you could've walked me out the door.
And been here with me.

"You are my foreword and all of my after thoughts.
I faint not waiting for you to be
what I know you will be."

*Unknown*

## DISTANCE

Do you hear me?
Feel me?
Palpitations.
Rhythmic patterns of connections,
perpetuation of nostalgia.
See me.
Know me.
Yearn me.
Want to be with me.
Let not time,
Nor person,
Nor place, separate.

# NO MAGICIANS

. . . . . .

Hogwarts created and spells handcrafted specifically for the specificity of cocoa brown, mocha, toffee, and vanilla-coated embryos to the full figured sweetly curved goddesses that can only be named as such.

Dipped in gold, we reign on land, in sea, creating seas in sheets and on desks meticulously calibrating functional organizational charts displaying the overwhelming ability to be magically delicious.

Yet these hands are in the flesh.
I see, feel, and have been bred in real time.
With real life issues.

It was not spells that procured my escape, but tears and heartache.

Plucked out of the line of fire, crawling under smoke filled lies, whimpering for a savior while the walls of life towered and tumbled.

Then, with no magic wand, took over sanctified altars of peace.

It was not magic, nor fairy tales that built the defense mechanisms that kept sarcasm, racism,

misogyny, and self-hatred from killing the
spark that my mother instilled deep in my psyche.

It was me.

It was definitive steps of intent, coupled with
night gazes, morning dreams, sharp 5am
morning breezes, and 2am back aches.

It was exhaustion and pointless relationships
that provided the stone foundation upon which
my hope has given my existence a home.

"Built destructively and poetically
to justify the eternal juxtaposition
of the arguments between he and me."

*Fixed*

## COLOR CODED DIFFERENCES

Speak.
Talk clearly.
Describe your experience with the hatred.
Don't cover it with white satin or cotton sheets.
Don't use words like affirmative, civil, religion, or oppression.

Don't repeat notions unproven.
Don't quote King James or Steve Bannon.

Tell me.
When were you last offended?
When were you denied the right because of a
right deemed just for someone else?

Have you ever had your dream stripped
mid REM sleep cycle while
battling pillows at 3am due to unforeseen
streams of pain replaying?

Tell me why my color upsets you.
What about my culture do you hate but love to take?
Create, rename, and discredit because ghetto is
trashy, but on manila complexions it's a trend.

Tell me.
Make me understand why bottles were thrown at my head.

Why was my tan so disgusting to you?

Yet you sit on fluorescent and ultraviolet lights

to achieve dark tones as seen in magazines
while turning your nose up to African Queens.

Who told you that you were superior because
your body lacks the proper amount of melanin
to be magnificently caramel?

Explain it to me so that I can share it with my unborn children.
Make it known, so that when your children hurt my children
I can better express my condolences to their innocence
for it will be quickly removed once their pure ears
understand this undeserved affliction.

Their play time will now harbor worry.
Then "don't shoot" will be next on their vocabulary quiz.

Help me understand why you hate yourself
and in turn hate my excellence so much.

## **EUPHORIA**

. . . . . .

Call me.
We Would.
Never thought.
Just maybe lately I have been pondering the possibility.
The idiosyncrasies that plague my senses.
Mental suffocations of your touch prelude me to a past time.
I consequently divulge all thought to focus in
On
On
On
And on, repetitively, to you.
Hazel facades, cascading down my cheek,
caressing even the finest hair present,
gently stroking my ego, leaving no room for
the timid to live.
You dive into my pores and glide beyond dreams,
insecurity,
doubt,
ambiguity
and exhale for me.
Call me Ah.
We would be.
Never thought this
Could capture my admiration,
shocking all sense of logic,
shaping this rhetoric circumstance,
not requiring explanation, definition, rhyme or reason.
It.
You.
I.

We evolve.
Peaking above mediocrity,
lurking beyond curiosity,
crawling and kneeling at the throne of its force,
power all given,
knowledge becoming,
Running from fear, misinterpretation, boastfulness, arrogance,
the light begins to shift.
My eyes began to see cyan blues and true magentas.
They glistened across my pupils and glared back at me.
Call me "ah love!"
We would be harmonious.
Never thought this could be.
Epitome of bliss, wrapped up in endearment, sealed with a kiss....

"A term handpicked for deception."

*Colors*

## ANOTHER MOMENT

Constant reminders
find us in a lethargic state of mind.
I sleep in your eyes and you rest in mine.
Mimicking the imitation of love I lie to myself.
Hidden yet,
obscure.
My fast-paced rhythm in my chambers unfold all truths.
Moistened palms.
Glistened glazes.
Euphoric touches.
Passionate phrases.
Doubts fly through the air like pollen and I chase them.
Chase them as if I were yellow and black, dying to devour the honey that resides,
blind to my high.
It still sits in my taste buds.
Relevance.
Ignorance.
Indulgence.
Dandelions implant themselves where ice conquered.
No longer, possibly.
Maybe.
Deep stares fade me.
Luminescent lost, unforgiving.
But yet reminiscent of a good moment that dissipated.
So, I wasted and I'll be waiting... I guess...

## DICTIONARY

. . . . . .

I search for words as I do my soul.
With intent.
Deliberate and with purpose.

Because the ones I have previously used
are bitter.
Tasting of twenty-nine-year-old milk.
Sitting in self-pity and poor reflections,
I need words that capture real experiences.

Words that define,
but not limit.
Describe, but not prohibit.

I need words like inhales and exhales.
Like light blue, shea butter, and hues.
I look for them as I look for the love from my past.
She and I were inseparable 'til thoughts parted.

She went as they did and I was left, here.
With essays and without instructions on life.
I need phrases to understand their meanings

I search for words as they do for me.

"And the honesty poured from his heart to the pen to the paper to the hereafter I tried to deny the truth."

**Can't Love**

## CONFESSIONS

Tell Me.
Pour Out Your heart.
Plaster your fears in the crimson of my soul.
Lay your worries deep.
And I will fill you with comfort.
Joy unspoken.
Into days unforeseen.

## DIRECT DECLARATIVE STATEMENTS

Fuck Taboo.
I mastered the game.
Yet, its presence in life left me stifled,
gasping for air and purpose.
Quiet murmurs of unachieved and unrealized
intangible dreams.
Societal norms don't suit my round ass.
So, I'd rather remain unapologetically
black, quirky, and present,
than be amazingly delicate and hidden.

"Paying homage to vintage thoughts..."

*Dress Up*

## TEMPORAL LOBE

Think of me and be mad.
Be upset that I'm present
only in your thoughts.
Tucked away like secret photos once delivered.
Think of our past and wonder.
Think of what is and what may not be,
but I ask you at least
just think of me.
Midday,
midway thru an important dialogue,
let my smile interrupt your speech.
Talk to me as you glare into the dark blue sky.
Speak as if I were there.

## 501, 22, 1 TOO MANY

. . . . . .

She left months prior.
"Left" they said.
Described her departure as a willful decision to part.
But they put her in a man-made cage built by
incapable of loving pieces of flesh.
Human at most, demons at best.

Yet runaway was her name instead of that given
by her drug addicted parents.
Bricks stood higher than the chance of peace ever did.

She left they said.
Runaway she said.

Slept on cold stone floors next to cold metal machines built to clean off the day of used garments for which she couldn't afford to even wear on any day.
Parted ways after the interview still in tears.
She was one for the 501, part of the 22, and 1 too many "runaways" I fear.

"She saw chipped paint on her surface
and assumed she was unfit for an upgrade."

*Divine*

## CONDITIONS MAY APPLY

You love me until my freedom threatens your wall.
Until my voice echoes louder than your ego
and pierces your ill-gotten pride.

You love the sound of my steps
until my footprints become a burden.

You desire me until my thoughts give life.
It's only then that I become a problem.
When my words aren't aligned with your
sentiments I become the enemy.

You love me until you can't control me.
Yet, you said you loved my liberation.

You said you loved my strength.
Maybe you just didn't like when I became
stronger than you.

When my determination carried a scent
and it swelled in your membranes,
redefining what you once thought I could
perform, forcing your preconceived notions to falter.

When conversations replayed
and memories crept up,
repeating things now lost to a former,
you no longer wanted to connect to me.

You preferred me in search of
that which was in search of synonyms of your declarations.
Pairings fit for a five course meal
of your liking.

Slanderous and dangerous were my opinions,
statements built upon experience that were of no value,
decreased as they left my tongue,
cut and chopped down before the next begun.

You created an imaginary battle to pin me against me,
then a war against you that I would never win.

But my enemy and your enemy are mirror
reflections of hate and discontent,
filled with foolish history misspoken by
human traffickers using religion and whips.

Because I now speak a language different than you
I am now the enemy too?

You praised my natural curls,
but rejected the Madame C J Walker to my tresses,
as if my blackness is to be proven,
tested, and out into a thesis,
Scientific method and corrected
to fit topics and concepts at your discretion.

It was then that I became the one for your dissection,
one you regretted professing.

## BAGGAGE

. . . . . .

I told you to leave.
I told you to stop communicating with my heart,
to stop reading my palms from miles away,
to stop knowing the right words to say.
I needed you to go.
I had to force myself to think without your baritone echoing in the chambers of my mind.
You read me like Langston Hughes, like Countee too.
You color me like the green leaves on Sycamore trees.
And when you left, I was unsure of my heart without it being connected to yours.
So you had to leave.
You need to be out of my memory.

"Your hunger beckoned me near,
I felt, internally."

***Served on a Platter***

## NOTE TO SELF

. . . . . .

You have the power.
Persistent.
Perfect.
Divine creation.
Gilded in excellence.
Yes, you have the power.

# THE SABBATH ON ANY GIVEN DAY

. . . . . .

Forgotten like vacant memories never desired,
assumptions flew that you and I don't speak.
But we talk in secret languages.

Built and guided from Nile-River-Deep connections,
we speak like kinfolk from decades of absence,
without the distance, apart.

Closest to my bosom.

Your name echoes in my trachea;
never foreign to me.

Remembered like secrets I wish to release.
Pillow talks.
Whispers.

Low and high pitches exchanged.
I talk to you like girlfriends on beaches sharing exhales
and expressing regrets of intimate undeserving

moments
with men-children now meddling somewhere between our

indifference and the unforgettable.
We talk as subconscious sounds invade my kinesphere.
You touch.

You heal.
You're here.
Closer than ever before.

Removed from edifices all over cities near liquor stores
with belief and contradictions alike
conversation never died.

Not changed.
Evolved as did your name.
And likewise, my soul.

"Please let me dive into shark-infested waters, jellyfish-saturated waves, killer-whale inhabited oceans, before..."

**Request Denied**

## BLACK LANDSCAPE 1

. . . . . .

Because it's all I knew.
Academia could've provided more information,
but I leaned on the jagged edges.
I followed the discomfort to undiscovered paths
and still ended up with it:
promises and dreams.
And words to fill them all up higher than
Liberty herself.
I tried to be a "good girl", but
broke bad and broke molds whenever my clench
was strong enough to carry and follow thru
and yet I still ended up,
here.

## BLACK LANDSCAPE 2

. . . . .

Fought hard and long.
Past time ended for new beginnings.
Created fortresses with bare hands in sculpted chests.
Mastered secret intentions.
Manifested and digested attempts to fortify
what did not bloom.

"You read me like Langston Hughes,
like Countee Cullen too."

*Baggage*

## LIFE LINE

. . . . . .

Take your smile,
plaster it inside my heart and let it
linger.

Stay in the comfort of my womb.
Build veins and become internally and eternally
mine.

Convert your footsteps
to follow my heartbeat and let us be
one.

## THE OLYMPIC COMMUTE

Against the wind,
with the weight of meetings, high expectations and low wages.

He cut the air with his body.
Starting point: taxi.
Finish line: desk job.

Over 40 in remarkable strides,
limbs pushing beyond limits of time and stamina,
flights of concrete,

glass windows not closer in actuality,
close to death,
closer to tumbling and crashing not made for real recovery.

The locomotive departs.
I'd hope they were present and accounted for as the train left.
Gasping for air, grateful for life they were.

"Your divinity isn't defined by the materials
on your back or by the style they're in.
You are divine simply because you inhale and exhale."

**_Queen_**

## SELF DEFENSE

Lie.
Lie down.
Lie down well.
Lie like tomorrow is never approaching.
Make believe you're honest.
Believe in fairy tales of integrity.
Tell me how real you are.
Lie to yourself.
With self-preservation in mind.

## BIG CHOP

I cut away all the death that surrounded me.

I took my place at the head of the table.

And I removed the labels.

I spoke down to misogyny.

And turned down contradictory doctrines.

Rejected notions built for captivity.

Denied access to hidden intentions.

Misread missions.

And enriched with hateful mentions.

"Beyond the pretty tides,
further than the outer reach"

*Love Me*

## RIGHTEOUS IN EVERY WAY YOU ARE

Because you are my everyday Sabbath.
My rest and peace.
Gratitude immersed in song.
Thankfulness covered in love.
I'd wait 6 days over and over for you.
Deep in mediation.
Sanctified praises unto your mother's womb.
I bask in the glory of your frame.
Divinity in your lips.
Kisses reminding me of grace and mercy,
you are holy.
Clothed and draped in excellence.
Because you are the blessed energy,
connectivity to the Creator in fact.
Definite purity in your steps.
As they cover the marble, gravel, or even plywood.
You are called by earthly terms but I see you
beyond belonging to clouds.
Fit for wings of gold and lily white.

## ON MY KNEES

. . . . . .

Let me beg.
Lead.
Bargain with eternity.
Offer up my peace and soul.
Just for the touch of your hand
upon my hips.

"Verbal assaults unto your heart and mind
attempting to push away what you told me was mine"

*Let You*

## LONG GONE

Do you miss me?
Did your thoughts take you places
unforeseen and reminiscent of us?
Did you miss me?
Did your dreams flood with my skin?
Did my voice and coos keep you up?

## DINNER TIME AT YOUR HOUSE

. . . . . .

Are you hungry?
Let me feed you.
Fixings liking to your palette.
Fit for a king.
Dine on me.
Get full of me.
Satisfy your taste buds.
Nectar so sweet.

"Cause I can't possibly love you.
Your middle name is a blur.
The interior decorations of your home never were."

*Infat*

## EMPTY SPACES

. . . . . .

Even with miles taunting our existence,
and time constantly rephrasing my persistence,
I can still taste the remembrance of you.
Folded like rose petals
withstanding decay,
firm in stature,
Hollowed in shadows dancing in my mind,
but never void.

## **WHERE THE WATER RAN**

. . . . . .

I found it all there,
whirl pooling at my feet
in solitude.

I didn't plan on succumbing to the urge,
the call,
the beckoning of the memories.

I was lulled in.
I stood firm as the pain let me go.
But then I found my knees bent.

So, I bathed in steam.
Poured scalding hot water down my back,
while wishing I knew voodoo to provoke your return.

Instead I watched memories, melodies, and words
follow the water down the drain,
leaving me unsatisfied and unanswered.

". . . . . ."

"Where hearts shattered, and were destroyed.

And there you stood..."

. . . . . .


***The Calm***

## PURPLE HAYES

. . . . . .

Thick clouds overhead don't matter to me now.
'Cause you are the only thing I need.
Your scent is a part of my soul.
Still giving me full control of you
no matter what I do.

## VOICE RECOGNITION IN LOVE

Because you like when I call you.
I address you with attention.
Confirm your heart's palpitations with touches to soothe.
Because you love it when I coo.
Sweet sounds and melodies.
Making declarations of your work down hallways,
bouncing off walls,
pitted against wooden frames and cotton pillows.
So I know it so.
Because you like it and love it.

"Lay your worries deep.
And I will fill you with comfort."

*Confessions*

## IN THE AFFIRMATIVE

Tried to talk down my self-love
and attempted to belittle the life left in my eyes,
hoping to strengthen his ill-gotten pride.
Came close to beating the communion out of my cries.
Managed to hide my tries
and kept me under his thumb long enough
for my self-reflection of appreciation to die.
And it was right then that I knew for this
misplaced love, to myself I could not lie.
So, I ran and set out for a piece of love's pie.

## FOR THE HISTORY BOOKS

And I still have evidence of your existence.
Occasionally surprising my heart,
recreating lapses in judgment.
I find you parked in recollections unrequited.
Keeping my feet bound to yesterday, yesterday.

Love letters never written.
Spoken in Pig Latin with good sex,
tested by fires too hot for consumption.
We stood until the heat scorched us.
Our attention, care, and obsession with this.

Four score and 7 days ago I reached for you.
Cried during meditation.
Saw your face in his.
Pretended to ignore your scent.
And dreamt I'd see you, walking, unmarried, and ready.

But you faded to glory.
And I found what you built buried.
And discovered what I crafted hidden.
Then felt us happy,
yet undeniably connected.

"I'd wait 6 days over and over for you"

*Sabbath*

www.ingramcontent.com/pod-product-compliance
Lightning Source LLC
LaVergne TN
LVHW051524070426
835507LV00023B/3295